The Peeling a Pomegranate

Hanukkah

Seder

by
Carly "Ketzirah" Lesser

First Printing: December 2012 (Kislev 5773)

www.thearils.com

Contact publisher for discounts on orders of 10 or more copies.
Email bulkorders@thearils.com for more information.

ISBN-13: 978-0615723938 (Arils, The)
ISBN-10: 0615723934

Cover design by Anastasia Vullis

Candle Lighting Poem by Rabbi Jill Hammer, used by permission of the author

Image Credits:
Cover Image via Shutterstock.com © Eugene Ivanov
Dreidels via Shutterstock.com, © LHG Graphics
Fish Plate via Shutterstock.com © Iestyan
Menorah (original) via Shutterstock.com © Eugene Ivanov
Menorah digital collage by Ketzirah
Olives via iStockPhoto.com © Sergio Bellotto
Wine and Cheese via Shutterstock.com © Pritmova Svetlana

Destruction of Leviathan".1865 engraving by GustaveDoré.
Public Domain Image, found at
http://commons.wikimedia.org/wiki/File:Destruction_of_Leviathan.png

Root Vegetables Botanical Drawing, Public Domain Image
found at vintageprintable.swivelchairmedia.com/

Judith and Holfernes by Andrea Mantegna, Public Domain Image
found at: http://etc.usf.edu/clipart/

Contents

Introduction

𝒲elcome to the Hanukkah Seder. Don't worry; you haven't been missing out on an ancient tradition. While there are several holidays that have a rich history of a seder as part of the celebration (Passover, Tu B'Shevat, and Rosh Hashanah), this is a new idea for Hanukkah. This seder is intended for the eighth night of Hanukkah, as all eighth candles are light during the seder, but I think you could also do it on the first night.

Hanukkah Seder Primer:

- **Themes**: Re/Dedication, Heroes/Heroines, Light in the Darkness, Power of the Individual, Things that are Hidden

- **Fours:** At Passover many things seem to come in fours. We have four cups, four questions, four children, and so on. At the Hanukkah seder, four is also an important number but appears in different ways, in stories we tell and courses we eat. In Jewish tradition the number four is symbolic of doorways, and I hope this seder is a doorway for you!

- **What's Hidden:** At Passover what is hidden is the Afikomen. Here at the Hanukah seder, what is hidden are different ideas that we need to uncover: things under the water, Jews in the Greek Empire and Pure Vial of Oil, The laws of nature and the sun, Judith's motives in camp of Holfernes.

- **Elements:** The four elements (earth, air fire, and water) are part of ancient Jewish mystical teachings. According to the teachings of Rabbi Jill Hammer, each season has an element in abundance and an element of need. The elements that are relevant during the winter and at Hanukah are Water (have) and Fire (need), and so are key aspects of this seder.

- **Candle Blessings:** All of the traditional Hanukkah candle blessings are included, but some are presented with alternative brachot and additional one has been created for this seder which is derived from the traditional Jewish prayer for the evening called, "maariv." Traditionally, we only say "Shehekianu" on the first night of Hanukkah, but it is included here because thematically it fits the experience, regardless of which night you use this seder.

- **Halakah:** Halakah is Jewish law, but it really means "the way." Some of us have a very proscribed way of practicing Judaism, others wander a bit more. This seder can and should be adapted to your observance of Halakah.

This seder is divided by dishes, not cups. So there is no separate section for the meal, it is integrated throughout the whole experience. The idea is to encourage you to eat, talk, and experience food, family and faith all together. As wine does not play as prominent a role in this seder as at Passover, there is no specific place to say a bracha over wine. If you choose to include wine, then I hope you will be sure to say the proper blessing (borei pri hagafen) before you drink your first cup.

Another change from the format of a Passover seder is that there are few specifications as to who should read what parts. I leave that to you to decide. You can designate certain parts for a leader or just go around the table having each person read a section.

You are also invited and encouraged to add your own special touches. Whether you want to play rounds of dreidel, sing songs, give gifts, or add your own readings to this seder – go for it. You'll find that I do recommend one additional reading, but feel free to find your own too.

There are also several Hanukkah songs included, but branch out and try including new Hanukkah songs that you can sing or listen to together. Try music by the Maccabeats or Matisyahu for a modern twist!

One other thing to mention that may be new to people. There has been a growing movement over the past twenty or so years to move away from "kingship" and gendered G!d/dess language to something that rings as more spiritually relevant to many people today. In the "brachot" (blessings), you'll find that I use the term "Ruach," which means Spirit or Breath, instead of "Melech," which means King. This is a common replacement in the Jewish Renewal movement and even in some of the other denominations. If you are more comfortable saying "Melech" then say "Melech!"

I hope you enjoy this Hanukkah seder. Much of this work is original, but of course much is inspired by other sources. Please see the bibliography for a list of sources used to create this work. Where others words were used directly, sources have been cited wherever possible.

I hope you'll share your experience using this Hanukkah Seder with me at peelapom.com or www.facebook.com/peelapom!

Happy Hanukkah,

The Seder

א. In The Beginning...

נֵס גָּדוֹל הָיָה שָׁם
Nes Gadol Hayah Sham

A Great Miracle Happened There
(Diaspora)

נֵס גָּדוֹל הָיָה פה
Nes Gadol Hayah Poh

A Great Miracle Happened Here
(Israel)

These are what the letters on the dreidel mean. Nun, Gimel, Hey, Shin (Peh) -- each stands for an idea. Once a year Jews are encouraged to put down the Torah and cease their studies because a great miracle happened here or there. We celebrate. We feast. We light lights that are only meant for beauty. Tradition tells us that the *chanukiyah* is not to be studied by, but just to be enjoyed for its beauty. Normally we are a frugal people. But here, at the darkest time of year we allow ourselves to relax and just enjoy the light.

Nes Gadol Chai Poh! A great miracle is alive here! Hanukkah is the celebration of a miracle long gone, but like Passover it must always be as though we lived the moment. So we say a great miracle lives here and now and weave our lives into the tradition.

Sevivion – Dreidel Song

Sevivon, sov, sov, sov
Hanukah, huchag tov
Hanukah, huchag tov
Sevivon, sov, sov, sov!

Hag simcha hu la-am
Nes gadol hayah sham
Nes gadol hayah sham
Hag simcha hu la-am.

סְבִיבוֹן סוֹב סוֹב סוֹב
חֲנוּכָּה הוּא חַג טוֹב
חֲנוּכָּה הוּא חַג טוֹב
סְבִיבוֹן סוֹב סוֹב סוֹב

חַג שִׂמְחָה הוּא לָעָם
נֵס גָּדוֹל הָיָה שָׁם
נֵס גָּדוֹל הָיָה שָׁם
חַג שִׂמְחָה הוּא לָעָם

Tonight we will join together to bring light from the darkness. We will eat, we will drink, we will laugh and play. Let us start by lighting the sun candle, for while many may call it a "shamash" or servant candle -- our shamash is symbol of the shemesh (sun)! Through our actions tonight we bring back the light.

Light the Shemesh Candle

יִתְרוֹמֵם לִבֵּנוּ, תְּשׁוֹבַב נַפְשֵׁנוּח, בְּהַדְלָקַת נֵר שֶׁל חֲנֻכָּה

Yitromeym libeynu, t'shovav nafsheynu, b'hadlakat neyr shel chanukkah

May our hearts be lifted and spirits refreshed as we light the Hanukkah (Tekufat Tevet – Winter Solstice) candles.

(light candle)

Read Together
We have crossed from the time of darkness to beginning of the rebirth of light. Tonight we re-kindle the light in our hearts as we pray for the light of the sun to return to our world.

Part I - The Great Leviathan

This is the season of water, but not necessarily gentle soothing water. This is the time of rains and heavy snow. This is the season when the world freezes over and icicles hang from our homes. At the same time, we need this time of harsh, cold water to ensure our crops will grow. The melted snow feeds the rivers. The hard freeze kills many of the bugs that would eat our crops. The Earth rests, but life in the sea continues.

> "On the fifth day of creation, G-d took fire and water, and out of these two elements He made the fishes of the sea. The animals in the water are much more numerous than those on land." [*Otzar haMidrashim, Hashem Bechachmah Yasad Aretz 6*]

Water and fire are the elements of this season. So we turn now to the sea -- to the Leviathan, the mythical sea monster. Tradition tells us that the Leviathan, a great (*gadol*) sea dragon was created as a playmate for the Elohim.

> "The ruler over the sea-animals is leviathan. With all the other fishes he was made on the fifth day...
>
> So enormous is leviathan that to quench his thirst he needs all the water that flows from the Jordan into the sea. His food consists of the fish which go between his jaws of their own accord. When he is hungry, a hot breath blows from his nostrils, and it makes the waters of the great sea seething hot....
>
> But leviathan is more than merely large and strong; he is wonderfully made besides. His fins radiate brilliant light, the very sun is obscured by it, and also his eyes shed such splendor that this marvelous beast is the plaything of G-d, in whom He takes His pastime." [*Otzar haMidrashim, Hashem Bechachmah Yasad Aretz 6*]

On the dreidel is the letter gimmel which stands for the word *gadol* (great). When we play the dreidel game, we get what's in the pot if on our turn it lands on gimmel.

> "G-d created the Leviathan. On every winter solstice, Leviathan would rear his head and make himself great and snort in the water and stir it up, and the fear of him would fall on all the fishes in the sea. If this were not so, the small could not stand before the great." [*Otzar haMidrashim, Hashem Bechachmah Yasad Aretz 6*]

As we spin the dreidel this Hanukkah, may we think of the great leviathan stirring things up and remember that each of us has the potential for greatness.

Light Two Candles

בָּרוּךְ אַתָּה יְיָ אֱלֹהֵינוּ רוּחַ הָעוֹלָם שֶׁהֶחֱיָנוּ וְקִיְּמָנוּ וְהִגִּיעָנוּ לַזְּמַן הַזֶּה

Baruch atah Adonai elohainu, ruach haolam, She-hekheyanu Ve-kiymanu Ve-higgi'anu La-zzman Ha-zzeh

Blessed are You, Holy One, Spirit of the World, who has kept us alive, preserved us, and enabled us to reach this season.

(light candles)

Read Together:
Let us bless the Source of Life who let nothing lack from this world and created in it beautiful creatures both great and small.

SERVE THE FIRST COURSE OF SOUP OR FISH

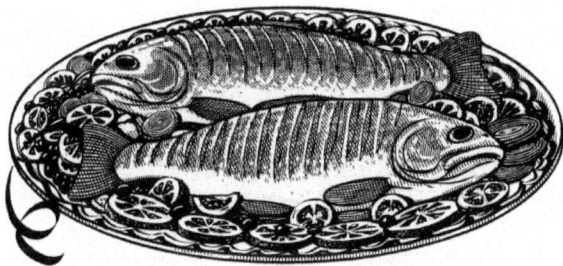

Blessing over the Food

בָּרוּךְ אַתָּה יְיָ אֱלֹהֵינוּ רוּחַ הָעוֹלָם שֶׁהַכֹּל נִהְיָה בִּדְבָרוֹ

Baruch atah Adonai elohainu, ruach haolam, shehakol nihyeh bi-d'varo

Blessed are You, Holy One, Spirit of the World,
At Whose Word all Things Come into Being.

*(Use this and any others appropriate
to the dishes, bread, or wine you serve)*

TELL BIG STORIES -- ESPECIALLY BIG FISH STORIES!

Part II - The Maccabee Miracle

In the winter the days grow shorter and we rely on fire more and more for its light and warmth. People light the outsides of their homes and place candles in the windows to ward of the darkness of the season. This season is also one where we need to work harder to keep our internal fires burning.

This is where the story of the Maccabees comes in. In the darkest days, when the people forgot who they were, stopped fighting and began acting more like Greeks than Hebrews -- a band of brothers stepped forward and fought back.

As we all know, they won the war and re-dedicated the Temple. That re-dedication alone is miraculous, but that was a very human-facing miracle. So, we have a second miracle to consider this time of year -- the miracle of the oil.

In a discussion of what kinds of candles may be used for Shabbat, one rabbi asks, rather casually, whether the rules for Hanukkah candles are different; in this context, another asks — as if he had barely heard of the festival — "What is this Hanukkah?"

And this is the answer he receives:

> "Our rabbis taught: On the 25th day of Kislev [begin] the eight days of Hanukkah, on which lamentation for the dead and fasting are forbidden. For when the Greeks entered the Temple, they defiled all the oils in it, and when the Hasmonean dynasty prevailed over them and defeated them, they searched and found only one bottle of oil sealed by the High Priest. It contained only enough for one day's lighting. Yet a miracle was brought about with it, and they lit [with that oil] for eight days. The following year they were established as a festival, with Hallel (prayers of praise) and Thanksgiving. [*Talmud Shabbat 21b*]

When the Maccabees re-dedicated the temple they did it through hard work and ritual. Maybe the rabbis of old wanted us to focus more on the hard work and perseverance it took to overcome great odds. The light lasting for eight days was only a part of the story and not the point of the story.

As we focus on what we need to re-dedicate ourselves to in our own lives, knowing that just speaking the words is not enough, take a moment to think about what you need to do to live more truly to who you are.

> ### Optional – Creative Readings
> This is a good place to add creative readings about the Maccabees, like the "Psalm of Mattathias." You can find a good translation in *A Blazing Fountain: A Book for Hanukkah,* by David Rosenberg and at http://jhom.com/calendar/kislev/psalms.html.

As we light the next two candles, let us re-dedicate the temples of our own body and souls. Know, as surely as the candles bring new light to this room, and as surely as you know the days will grow longer that this flame can grow brighter within yourself, with a little work and dedication.

Light Two Candles

בָּרוּךְ אַתָּה יְיָ אֱלֹהֵינוּ רוּחַ הַעוֹלָם שֶׁעָשָׂה נִסִּים
לַאֲבוֹתֵינוּ בַּיָּמִים הָהֵם בַּזְּמַן הַזֶּה

Baruch atah adonai, Eloheinu Ruach HaOlam, She-asa nee-seem la-avo-teinu v'emateinu Baya-meem ha-haim baz-man ha-zeh.

Blessed are You, Holy One, Spirit of the World, who wrought miracles for our forefathers and foremothers, in those days at this season.

(light candles)

Read Together:

We are grateful for miracles great and small, past, present and future that light the way for our ancestors, ourselves and our children. Now we will enjoy dishes made of olives and olive oil to remind of the miracle of oil, the miracle of light, the miracle of fire, and the miracle of the power a small group of dedicated people.

Mi Yimalel (Traditional Song)

Who can retell the things that befell us, Who can count them? In every age, a hero or sage Came to our aid.	מִי יְמַלֵּל גְּבוּרוֹת יִשְׂרָאֵל אוֹתָן מִי יִמְנֶה הֵן בְּכָל דּוֹר יָקוּם הַגִּיבּוֹר גּוֹאֵל הָעַם
Hark! In days of yore in Israel's ancient land Brave Maccabees lead a faithful band And now all Israel must as one arise Redeem itself through deed and sacrifice	שְׁמַע בַּיָּמִים הַהֵם בַּזְּמַן הַזֶּה מַכַּבִּי מוֹשִׁיעַ וּפוֹדֶה וּבְיָמֵינוּ כָּל עַם יִשְׂרָאֵל יִתְאַחֵד, יָקוּם וְיִגָּאֵל

Miyimalel gvurot Yisrael,
Otan mi yimne?
Hen be'chol dor yakum ha'gibor
Goel ha'am!

Shma!
Ba'yamim ha'hem ba'zman ha'zeh
Maccabi moshia u'fode
U'v'yameinu kol am Yisrael
Yitached yakum ve'yigael!

SERVE THE SECOND COURSE OF OLIVE-BASED DISHES

Blessing over the Food

בָּרוּךְ אַתָּה יְיָ אֱלֹהֵינוּ רוּחַ הָעוֹלָם בּוֹרֵא פְּרִי הָעֵץ

Baruch atahadonai, ruach ha-olam, borei-prei ha-Eitz.

Blessed are You, Holy One, Your Presence fills the World
Forming the Fruit of the Tree

(Use this and any others brachot appropriate to the dishes you serve)

TELL STORIES OF MIRACLES BOTH LARGE AND SMALL!

Part III - Adam at the Solstice

Now we must wonder, is there more to this story than we have been told? How deep do the roots of this holiday go if we dig deeper? Will we find more below the surface?

Hanukkah falls at the junction of the Winter Solstice and the New Moon. Surely, our ancestors had the Winter Solstice in mind during this time of year. Surely, the progressive building of lights during this holiday must relate to slow return of light after the Winter Solstice.

> "When Adam saw the day gradually diminishing, he said, "Woe is me! Perhaps because I offensively, the world around me is growing darker and darker, and is about to return to chaos and confusion, and this is the death heaven has decreed for me."
>
> He then sat eight days in fast and prayer.But when the winter solstice arrived, and he saw the days getting gradually longer, he said, "Such is the way of the world," and proceeded to observe eight days of festivity. The following years he observed both the eight days preceding and the eight days following the solstice as days of festivity." [*Babylonian Talmud, Avodah Zarah 8a*]

But we also see in other stories that Adam feared the changing light not just this once. In this first story, set at the solstice, Adam is alone, but in another story of the disappearing sun Chava (Eve) is also present.

> "When Adam on the day of creation saw the sun sinking in the sky before him, he said, "Woe is me! Because I acted offensively, the world is darkening for me and is about to return to darkness and desolation--indeed, this is the death that Heaven has decreed for me."
>
> So he sat down to fast and to weep through the night, while Eve wept beside him.

But when the dawn began slowly rising like a column, he said, "Such is the way of nature, and I did not realize it," and then proceeded to offer up a bullock."
[*Babylonian Talmud, AvodahZarah 8a*]

What are the roots of these stories and what can we learn from them? Twice Adam experiences a similar thing, only to react with fear and then learn it is only the way of the world. As we light the next two candles, let us remind ourselves of the deeper roots of truth that we may forget in moments of change in our own lives.

Light Two Candles

בָּרוּךְ אַתָּה יְיָ אֱלֹהֵינוּ רוּחַ הַעוֹלָם
פּוֹתֵחַ שְׁעָרִים מְשַׁנֶּה עִתִּים

Baruch atah adonai, eloheinu ruach ha-olam
poteach shearim me-sha-neh' i-tim

Blessed are You, Holy One, Your Presence fills Creation,
Which Opens the Gates and Changes the Seasons.

(light candles)

Hanukkah Candle Lighting
By RK'Jill Hammer

Light born from darkness,
Dawn born from night,
Hope born from quiet
Waiting for the light.

Spring born from winter,
Spark struck from sun,
Strength born from calling
For the spring to come.

Tonight the dark is waiting,
Longing to be gone.
Tonight the earth is turning,
Facing toward the dawn.

Original melody by Ketzirah
http://snd.sc/QEbs3d

SERVE THIRD COURSE OF ROOT VEGETABLES

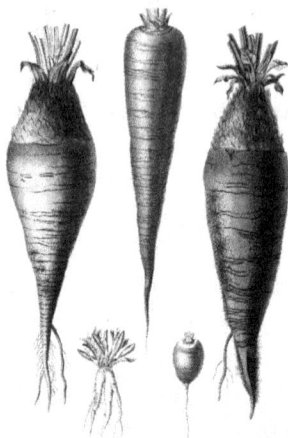

Blessing over the food:

בָּרוּךְ אַתָּה יְיָ אֱלֹהֵינוּ רוּחַ הָעוֹלָם
בּוֹרֵא פְּרִי הָאֲדָמָה

Baruch ataha donai, eloheinu ruach ha-olam,
borei prei haAdamah.

Blessed are You, Holy One, Your Presence fills Creation
Forming the Fruit of the Earth.

(Use this and any others appropriate to the dishes you serve)

TELL STORIES OF THE EARTH, ROOTS, AND HOW THE WORLD WORKS!

Part IV - Judith

𝒲e end our journey tonight with the story of Yehudit (Judith); the story of one woman who saw and acted. She acted when no one else would to save her people. Judith is a true Hanukkah and solstice story, because it is the story of seeing the light in the darkness and personal dedication to action.

As Rabbi Jill Hammer says, "The Book of Judith is, after all, a story of the triumph of one small person over an army— a little light illuminating the darkness."

The Story of Judith
(Original adaptation from the Book of Judith)

> The town of Bethulia was besieged by the great General Holfernes and legions of soldiers. The town's people suffered and were terrified that they would be taken captive or killed. In the town there was a beautiful learned widow named Yehudit, daughter of a prophet, who devised a plan to help her people.
>
> When no one else seemed to see a light in the darkness, she found a way. She dressed in her most beautiful clothes and jewels, for the first time since her husband had died more than three years earlier. She told her maidservant to prepare a basket with wine, oil, parched corn, dry figs, cheeses, and bread to take to the camp of the General.
>
> When Yehudit and her maidservant reached the gates of Bethulia, the leaders of the town were there. The men were dumbstruck not only by Yehudit's beauty, but also by her bravery. As they opened the gates and let Yehudit and her maidservant pass through they said, "The G-d of our fathers give thee grace, and may he strengthen all the counsel of thy heart with his power, that Jerusalem may glory in thee, and thy name may be in the number of the holy and just." [*Book of Judith 10:8*]

When Yehudit and her maidservant reached the camp of General Holfernes they were stopped by the guards, who asked who they were and what they were doing there.

Yehudit answered, "I am a daughter of the Hebrews, and I fled from them, because I knew they would be made a prey to you, because they despised you, and would not of their own accord yield themselves, that they might find mercy in your sight. For this reason I thought: I will go to the presence of the prince Holofernes, that I may tell him their secrets, and show him by what way he may take them, without the loss of one man of his army." [*Book of Judith 10:12-13*]

The guards were so mesmerized by Yehudit's beauty that they took her directly to the General, who was also stunned by her beauty and invited her to dine with him. Yehudit was careful to only eat what her maid had prepared for her, but she encouraged Holfernes to eat and drink more and more. He ate bread and salted cheese and drank more and more wine to slake his thirst, and in time, quite drunk and fell into a stupor.

And when it was very late and all the servants had retired to their chambers, Yehudit was alone with General Holfernes in his drunken sleep. She gathered her courage and prayed, "O Lord G-d of all power, Strengthen me, O Lord G-d of Israel, this day." [*Book of Judith 13:4-7*] When the prayer was finished she took Holfernes' sword from where it lay and, with two blows, severed his head from his body.

Yehudit and her maidservant placed the head in a bag and fled the General's camp for the city gates. When the leaders of the city saw her they believed she had failed.

Yehudit produced the head of Holfernes and said, "Praise ye the Lord our G-d, who hath not forsaken them that hope in him. And by me his handmaid he hath fulfilled his mercy, which he promised to the house of Israel: and he hath killed the enemy of his people by my hand this night." [*Book of Judith 13:17-18*]

The leaders of the city were stunned and and the Prince declared, "Blessed art thou, O daughter, by the Lord the most high G-d, above all women upon the earth." [*Book of Judith 13:23*]

At first light, it was discovered in the General's camp that he had been slain. Without him, his armies lost their courage and retreated as quickly as they could leaving all behind. Bethulia was saved.

Here we have the story of Judith. What do you think of it? What is the moral of this story? Let us silently light the final two candles in memory of all those brave women and men whose personal sacrifices and dedication have helped to save us from tyrants.

Light Two Candles

The final two candles are lit in silence.

(light candles)

READ TOGETHER:

We end our evening's journey enjoying cheese and wine to honor the individual acts and sacrifices that change the world for the better.

נֵס גָּדוֹל הָיָה שָׁם	נֵס גָּדוֹל הָיָה פֹּה
Nes Gadol Hayah Sham	*Nes Gadol Hayah Poh*
A Great Miracle Happened There (Diaspora)	A Great Miracle Happened Here (Israel)

Al Hanissim (Traditional Song)

Al hanissim v'al hapurkan
V'al hagvurot V'al hot'shuot
V'al hanifla'ot she'asita la'avoteinu
Bayamim hahem bizman hazeh

עַל הַנִּסִּים, וְעַל הַפֻּרְקָן
וְעַל הַגְּבוּרוֹ, וְעַל הַתְּשׁוּעוֹת
וְעַל הַנִּפְלָאוֹת, שֶׁעָשִׂיתָ לַאֲבוֹתֵינוּ
בַּיָּמִים הָהֵם בִּזְמַן הַזֶּה

Translation
[We thank You G-d] For the miracles, the redemption,
the mighty acts, the saving acts and for the wonders
that You have done for our fathers, in those days at this time.

READ TOGETHER:

לְעָלַם וּלְעָלְמֵי עָלְמַיָּא, וְאִמְרוּ : אָמֵן
Le'olam ulmay almaya, v'eimeru: amen

In this world, in all the worlds, we say: Amen.

SERVE FOURTH COURSE OF CHEESE AND ENJOY.

Blessing over the Food

בָּרוּךְ אַתָּה יְיָ אֱלֹהֵינוּ רוּחַ הַעוֹלָם שֶׁהַכֹּל נִהְיָה בִּדְבָרוֹ

Baruch atahadonai, eloheinu ruach ha-olam shehakol nihyah bidvaro

Blessed are You, Holy One, Spirit of the World,
through Whose word everything comes into being.

*If you are drinking wine with this course and have not yet
said the bracha for wine, include this here*

בָּרוּךְ אַתָּה יְיָ אֱלֹהֵינוּ רוּחַ הַעוֹלָם בּוֹרֵא פְּרִי הַגָּפֶן

Baruch atah Adonai elohainu, ruach haolam, borei pri hagafen

Blessed are You, Holy One, Your Presence fills the World
Forming the Fruit of the Vine.

(Use this and any others appropriate to the dishes you serve)

TELL STORIES OF BRAVERY AND CLEVERNESS TO DEFEAT OPPRESSION!

Birkat Hamazon

In Jewish tradition we say "bracha" before we eat, but give thanks after we eat with prayers called "Birkat Hamazon," or grace after the meal. Below is my original take on Birkat Hamazon. Feel free to use this, traditional texts, or songs of your choosing!

Read Together

We bless those that turned the earth!
We bless those that planted the seed!
We bless those that watered the fields!
We bless those that tended the livestock!
We bless those that harvested the crops!
We bless those that brought the harvest to market!
We bless those that prepared the meal!

וְאָכַלְתָּ, וְשָׂבָעְתָּ--וּבֵרַכְתָּ אֶת-יְיָ אֱלֹהֶיךָ,
עַל-הָאָרֶץ הַטֹּבָה אֲשֶׁר נָתַן-לָךְ

V'achalta V'savata U'veirachata et Adonai Elohecha al Ha'aretz Hatova Asher Natan Lach

We have eaten, and are satisfied, and so we bless the Holy One
for the good Earth we have been given
and all those that enabled this food to reach our table.

Food Notes

Fish/Soup: Classic gefilte fish will do just fine here, but if it's cold where you live you may want to choose a nice hot soup or a fish dish. <u>Saffron Shores</u>, a cookbook of Mediterranean Jewish cooking has many wonderful and exotic fish dishes and soups.

Olives: Latkes count here, if you fry them in olive oil! Or you could serve good, artisan bread and dip it in olive oil or even just olive bread. You could also have a selection of cured olives for your guests to try. If you serve bread, please be sure to say "hamotzei!"

Root Vegetables: Root vegetables were chosen because they are in season in many parts of the world in the winter, and are symbolic of the roots we dig into when we tell all the stories of Hanukkah. Potatoes are certainly root vegetables, so if you didn't serve Latkes in the olive course, you may want to here. Roasted root vegetables are delicious and you can find many reliably delicious recipes on websites like Epicurious.com. Also, you may want to try experimenting with Sunchokes (if they are in season near you), which are also called Jerusalem Artichokes. The correspondence with the sun and Jerusalem make them a perfect food to serve.

If you aren't used to vegetarian cooking, check out Simple Suppers or any cookbook from Moosewood Collective (see resources on the next page). They have great recipes that are very reliable!

Try to explore interesting combinations of root vegetables like Purple Potatoes and Fennel (see next page for resources), which sounds like a great recipe for this section.

Cheese: Americans don't really do cheese as a dessert dish, except for cheesecake, but it's common in other cultures. Just go to your local cheese shop, and I'm sure they can help you put together a nice selection. Try mango stilton if you can find it. It's delicious! Where's the meat? Well, as there is cheese at the end of the meal it wouldn't be kosher! If you don't follow traditional kashrus and just can't live without the meat, I would recommend serving it with the root vegetables. Please consider choosing local, sustainable, cruelty-free meats.

Food Blessings: Depending on your style of observance, the blessings as listed in this seder may not be appropriate for you. Please use your own judgment as to which blessings you need to use to ensure you maintain kashrus to your own standards.

Recipe Resources

- **Saffron Shores: Jewish Cooking of the Southern Mediterranean**: http://ow.ly/J0eO
- **The Scent of Orange Blossoms: Sephardic Cuisine from Morocco**: http://ow.ly/J0fp
- **Moosewood Restaurant Simple Suppers: Fresh Ideas for the Weeknight Table**: http://ow.ly/J0fW
- **Cheese & Wine: A Guide to Selecting, Pairing, and Enjoying**: **http://ow.ly/J0gE**
- Purple Potatoes and Fennel: http://ow.ly/fKhq3

Bibliography & Sources

Adam and the Solstice
http://telshemesh.org/tevet/jewish_winter_solstice_tales.html

Brachot
Book of Blessings, Marcia Falk
The Path of Blessing, Marcia Prager
Kohenet Siddur, RK'Jill Hammer & K'Taya Shere
http://en.wikipedia.org/wiki/List_of_Jewish_prayers_and_blessings
http://www.chabad.org/library/article_cdo/aid/278538/jewish/Basic-Blessings-on-Food-Guide.htm

Hanukkah
http://en.wikipedia.org/wiki/Chanukkah
http://www.jhom.com/calendar/kislev/hebrew.html
http://www.chabad.org/library/article.asp?AID=98951

General
Sefer Ha-Aggadah: The Book of Legends
Hayim Nahman Bialik and Yehoshua Hana Ravnitzky (editors) Schocken Books, New York, 1992

Judith
http://telshemesh.org/tevet/chanukah_and_the_olive_harvest.html
http://www.hillel.org/jewish/textstudies/holidays/judith.htm
http://www.chabad.org/magazine/article_cdo/aid/64493/jewish/Judith.htm

Lamps & Light Stories
http://www.jhom.com/calendar/kislev/proverbs.htm

Leviathan
http://www.jhom.com/topics/fish/leviathan.html

Maccabees
http://jewishencyclopedia.com/articles/10236-maccabees-the
http://jewishencyclopedia.com/view.jsp?artid=351&letter=H
http://jewishencyclopedia.com/view.jsp?artid=672&letter=J
http://jewishencyclopedia.com/view.jsp?artid=263&letter=M
http://www.jhom.com/calendar/kislev/psalms.html
A Blazing Fountain: A Book for Hanukkah, David Rosenberg (NY: Schocken Books)

Miracle of the Oil

http://www.jhom.com/calendar/kislev/origins.ht
Seasons of Our Joy: A Celebration of Modern Jewish Renewal,
Beacon Press, 1992.

Shamash

http://en.wikipedia.org/wiki/Shamash
http://www.windows.ucar.edu/tour/link=/mythology/shamash_sun.html
http://www.milon.co.il/dictionary/english-to-hebrew.php?term=shemesh-
http://alexm.here.ru/mirrors/www.enteract.com/jwalz/Eliade/133.html

Songs

http://www.chabad.org/multimedia/media_cdo/aid/218974/jewish/Chanukah-Songs.htm
http://www.zemirotdatabase.org/view_category.php?id=9
https://soundcloud.com/peelapom/jewish-solstice-song

About the Author

My name is Carly Lesser
(a.k.a. Ketzirah – קְצִירָה), and I am
a Kohenet, Artist and Ritualist. I
work with individuals and groups
to explore, discover, and create
meaningful rituals and ritual
artwork to mark life's moments –
from personal moments and
holiday celebrations to weddings,
baby namings, and life transitions.

My passion is helping Jews who are unaffiliated, earth-based or in
interfaith / inter-denominational relationships connect more deeply with
Judaism and make it relevant in their everyday lives.

You can learn more at www.peelapom.com and find me at
facebook.com/peelapom and twitter.com/peelapom

Other Books by Ketzirah
- Ruby Red Seeds, A Collection of Poetry Prayer and Midrash;
  Available on Amazon.com
- The Peeling a Pomegranate Passover Seder;
  Currently available at http://peelapom.etsy.com and
  available on Amazon.com Spring 2013

www.ingramcontent.com/pod-product-compliance
Lightning Source LLC
Chambersburg PA
CBHW060647030426
42337CB00018B/3484